T0156827

ITALY
CENTRAL

Italy
Central

Abruzzo Travel Guide -
The True Italia

Rock DiLisio

ITALY CENTRAL
ABRUZZO TRAVEL GUIDE - THE TRUE ITALIA

Copyright © 2011 by Rock DiLisio.

Editor: Brianna Flasco
Contributor: Luciano DiSalle (Raiano, Italy)

iUniverse books may be ordered through booksellers or by contacting:

iUniverse
1663 Liberty Drive
Bloomington, IN 47403
www.iuniverse.com
1-800-Authors (1-800-288-4677)

Because of the dynamic nature of the Internet, any web addresses or links contained in this book may have changed since publication and may no longer be valid. The views expressed in this work are solely those of the author and do not necessarily reflect the views of the publisher, and the publisher hereby disclaims any responsibility for them.

Any people depicted in stock imagery provided by Thinkstock are models, and such images are being used for illustrative purposes only.
Certain stock imagery © Thinkstock.

ISBN: 978-1-4620-6374-1 (sc)
ISBN: 978-1-4620-6375-8 (e)

Print information available on the last page.

iUniverse rev. date: 05/31/2018

CONTENTS

CHAPTER 1

Abruzzo—The *True* Italy

Piazza Garibaldi and medieval aqueduct – Sulmona

The Italy of one's imagination is envisioned as one encompassing the numerous tourist meccas, which have delighted and entertained countless visitors over the past century. The cities of Rome, Florence, Venice, Milan and Naples are recognized by even the least of worldly travelers, and the same can be said of the famous regions, such as Tuscany and Lombardia. Italy simply has a vast array of cultural and topographical locations to enthrall and tantalize even the most skeptical of travelers. After all, it's not often that you encounter someone who did not enjoy their visit to *Italia*.

If someone where to ask, "Where can I go to see the *true* Italy?"—What would be the response? This is a difficult question to answer, because even near the tourist meccas sit smaller locales that are seemingly unscathed by the throng of travelers. Life goes on there, as it has for millennia and it will continue too. The typical answer to the question, though, would be the Province of Abruzzo.

This is not at all surprising considering that the name "Italia" or "Italy" originated in Abruzzo. "*The name Italia was imposed upon the Roman Republic by the conquering Italic tribes of the contemporary Abruzzo region, centering in the area of Corfinium (Corfinio).*"

Abruzzo is located in east/central Italy and is approximately 50 miles due east from Rome and offering the exquisite flavor of ancient roman culture. It is primarily bordered by the Adriatic Sea to the east, and the Apennine Mountains to its west. Abruzzo also borders the region of Marche to the north, Molise to the south-east and Lazio to the west. Without question, Abruzzo is located in one of the most mountainous regions in all of Italy. The Apennines include the tallest peak on the Italian peninsula, the Gran Sasso, and Europe's southernmost glacier, the Calderone.

The winding Apennine mountain range is what creates the imposing physical, and yet imaginary border between the Italy we all know and the Italy we truly want to experience. Nestled on the eastern side of the Apennines is the region of Abruzzo, seemingly forgotten by the average tourist. While in Italy, tourists often seek the major cities and regions of known popularity, neither of which Abruzzo offers in abundance. Though this is the case, this happenstance has now evolved into a tourist destination of a different sort.

The Abruzzo region is considered by many to be remote and mountainous. The Apennines have been an obstacle for travelers not wanting to drive the high, winding mountainous roads, which are the primary, and sometimes the only, entry points to the province. Travelers have skirted the region for centuries in search of smoother lanes of travel, which they find in abundance.

The isolation of the region, though, is now considered by many to be "God's Country," where you can find some of the least visited cities and hill towns in all of Italy. This is why Abruzzo is considered the "True Italy," where the average Italian toils in his/her daily life, where old-world traditions still reign, all without the overwhelming monetary influence of the tourist. Though tourism has increased over the years, Abruzzo is still an area visited primarily by other Italians and various Europeans. The interest in Abruzzo steadily increases with each passing year as tourists are attracted to the region for its rich cluster of castles and its medieval heritage towns. Over the past decades, tourism in Abruzzo has increased, again primarily among Italians and other Europeans. Abruzzo's wealth of castles and medieval towns has led it to be called by the nickname of "Abruzzoshire" by many. This nickname is a reference to the analogy with the "Chiantishire" nickname, often used to refer to the *Chianti* area of *Tuscany*. Still, even with the increased influx of tourism, Abruzzo is still off the beaten path for most visitors to Italy.

Whether you like the seashore or the mountains, river valleys or ancient towns, Abruzzo has something pleasing for everyone and is a region rich of work and culture, of history and activities. The purpose of this book is to be a guide into the heart of Italy, Abruzzo, to cities and towns not typically heard of and where life is sometimes as untouched and golden as it was in centuries past.

CHAPTER 2

Location and Geography
of Abruzzo

Raiano – Natural beauty of Abruzzo near Raiano

Abruzzo is a region of Italy (one of 20), which has its most western border lying approximately less than 50 miles due east of Rome. It is geographically located in central Italy, but its southern borders stretch into what many consider the southern region of the country. The region of Marche borders Abruzzo to the north, Molise to the south-east and Lazio to the west and south-west. Its location on the Italian peninsula has it facing the Adriatic Sea to the east and the Apennine Mountain range to the west. The combination of seaside and mountain range environments, in the same region, is an unusual combination of landscapes.

The territory is roughly semi-circular and has a diameter of approximately 93 miles or 150 kilometers. The entire region is 6,707 miles or 10,794 square kilometers and it contains 305 municipalities.

The Abruzzo region has an attractive coastline stretching along the Adriatic seashore. The region has 93 miles

(150 kilometers) of sandy shoreline and pebbly beaches overlooked by tree-covered hills. The area is also known for its high, jagged cliffs and narrow creeks all encompassed in a coastline of beautiful beaches and resort towns.

A majority of the Abruzzo territory is mountainous with some calculations approximating it to encompass 65 percent of the region, though half of that percentage may be deemed hills. There are a series of mountain ranges or chains, primarily in the western half of Abruzzo. They include Majella, Corno Grande, Simbruini, Laga, Gran Sasso, Sirente, Velino, Monte Mariscani and Ernici. As mentioned previously, the Apennines include the tallest peak on the Italian peninsula, the Gran Sasso, and Europe's southernmost glacier, the Calderone. Throughout Abruzzo, every now and then you can catch a glimpse of a glistening chain of mountains culminating in a solitary and mighty peak. This is the *Gran Sasso d'Italia* whose summits are 8,200 feet or 2500 meters, and at other points, such as in the case of Corno Grande, 9,850 feet or 3000 meters. The Gran Sasso massif creates the Italian peninsula's highest peak, Corno Grande, and as mentioned earlier, Europe's southernmost glacier, Il Calderone.

The winding Apennines consistently offer towering peaks and highlands that include lush landscapes of waterfalls, caves and woodlands. Their formidable crests and cliffs and magnificent alpine characteristic outlines creates a dolomitic appearance.

The Vomano, Alterno-Pescara, Salinello and Sangro Rivers have opened up passes through these mountain chains creating beautiful gorges, as they slice their way towards the Adriatic. The Abruzzo region is not known for its lakes, but is home to the beautiful Lake Scanno and a number of smaller lakes, namely, Pantaniello, Barrea, Campotosto and Bomba.

CHAPTER 3

Abruzzo Weather

Italy, in general, has what many proclaim as the *"best weather in the entire world."* It boasts a mild Mediterranean climate with warm average temperatures and sunny skies. The average summer temperatures are between 79 to 87 degrees Fahrenheit.

Abruzzo, due to its vast differential in topography, has two climate systems: maritime and continental. The climate may be termed warm and dry on the coast and an alpine climate in the mountainous region. The annual average temperature is 53-60 degrees Fahrenheit in the maritime (Seashore) zone (12-16 degrees Celsius) and 46-54 degrees Fahrenheit (8-12 degree Celsius) in the inland and mountain regions.

Abruzzo's mountainous 'continental' thermal temperature is always lower due to its natural air conditioning system. The Apennines let out heat during the night, counteracting the lower temperatures caused by the higher altitudes.

The summer months boast an average temperature of 75 degrees Fahrenheit (24 degrees Celsius) on the maritime coastline and 68 degrees (20 degrees Celsius) on the inland continental basin. Temperatures often are in the 80's (Fahrenheit), with some mild periods of humidity. The climate, however, is typically dry.

There can be a great variation of daily temperature changes, in particular, between temperatures during the day and those at night. This is caused by a combination of altitude in the elevated basins and general thermal changes. Hot days and cooler nights are not uncommon. The coldest month is January, when the average temperature on the coastline-seashore dips, on average, to 46 degrees Fahrenheit or 8 degrees Celsius. It has been known to drop to at least

32 degrees Fahrenheit or zero Celsius in the inland region and, in particular, the mountainous zones.

Rainfall varies by location with the least amount occurring during the summer and the most being noticed during the month of November. Throughout the year, Abruzzo has very few days of constant rain. November is the wettest month and spring is punctuated by short, heavy showers. Between mid-June and mid-September, there is the occasional spectacular storm, but otherwise little rain.

During the winter months, snow may accumulate in varying amounts in the lower elevations, typically not in abundance, nor remaining on the ground for long. In winter, there is enough snow at times to be scenic, but not enough to be a nuisance (The roads get cleared very efficiently). Though it gets cold, the temperature rarely stays below freezing. In the mountains, the snowfall often remains anywhere between one to six months and, in the case of the peak of the Corno Grande, throughout the year.

CHAPTER 4

Tourism—Seaside Resorts of Abruzzo

Abruzzo is blessed to have almost 100 miles of shoreline, which gracefully curves along the Adriatic Sea. The long, sandy coastline is home to many popular beach resorts and dramatic maritime views. Abruzzo actually offers a coastline for all tastes, including wide, sandy shores, pebbly beaches and others with a mix of grass and vegetation. The beaches of Abruzzo are truly a heaven and are very famous for their selection of gelato and very busy restaurants specializing in a great assortment of flavorful fish.

Some of the most popular beach resort areas include **Pescara**, **Alba Adriatica**, **Vasto** and **Silvi Marina**.

Beaches of Pescara

Pescara

Pescara is a very modern coastal city, which has its climate often influenced by the surrounding Maiella and Gran Sasso mountain ranges. During the summer months, the weather is mostly sunny with comfortable temperatures and a slight sea breeze. The city is famous for its 6.5 mile long wide sandy beaches with seaside promenade. Pescara is one of the most popular seaside resort cities along the entire Adriatic Coast, with an abundance of restaurants, stylish outdoor discos, shopping districts, fashion boutiques and night life.

Pescara is also considered the "major" city of the entire Abruzzo region, and is certainly one of the most important in terms of tourism, commercial and economic factors. It has its own airport and three train stations, including the largest in Abruzzo and one of the largest in Europe-Pescara Centrale. In the historic center of the city, interesting sites include the Cathedral of St. Cetteus (famous for Guercino paintings) and the Basilica of Madonna dei Sette Dolori—which is a sanctuary, built on the location of several Marian apparitions. It's also the home of the Museum of the Abruzzi people, which traces their 4,000 years of history.

Alba Adriatica

Alba Adriatica is located in the Province of Teramo (northern Abruzzo coast) and it is one of the so-called "seven sisters"—resort towns along the northern Abruzzo coast. The other "sisters" include: Pineto, Roseto degli Abruzzi, Martinsicuro, Giulianova, Tortoreto and Silvi Marina (see below).

Alba Adriatica is known for its beaches being edged by Pinewood and an absolute abundance of hotels and villas. It has high quality beaches, which has earned it the nickname of *Spiaggia d'argento* or *Silver Beach*. The high quality of the area has earned it the European Blue Flag award at least four times in the recent past.

Vasto Marina

Vasto and Vasto Marina is a city perched on a cliff and is sometimes called the "Sea-Side Pearl of the Adriatic." This relaxing, family-friendly and beautiful sea-side resort town is located on Abruzzo's southern coast. Vasto Marina is filled with splendid views, very nice stretches of sand and beaches and also some mountainous backcountry. The small, coastal town also includes good restaurants, medieval buildings and other attractions.

Silvi Marina

Located at the point where Teramo meets Pescara, Silvi has a 4 kilometer (2.5 mile) long beach and an abundance of cultural and entertainment venues, including nightclubs, sports scene and hotels. It must be mentioned that Silvi Marina's sand is considered among the best in Italy. Abruzzo is also home to what is called the *Sette Sorelle* or Seven Sisters. These are seven seaside resorts located in the Province of Teramo. Pineto and Silvi Marina are a couple of the resorts, but others include **Martinsicuro**, with its wide, sandy beaches, and **Francavilla al Mare**. All of these northern Abruzzo resorts offer excellent accommodations, restaurants and nightclubs.

Other Notable Abruzzo
Seaside Resort Areas

Other seaside resorts include, **Marina di Citta' San Angelo**, which has pebbly beaches and also its share of vegetation, **Pineto**, which is known for having Pinewood right on its beaches, and **Tortoreto Lido**, which has beaches adorned with palms and pines. Another resort town, **Giulianova**, is known for its beautiful beaches and boating and for being a primary tourist area for people from major cities such as Rome and Milan, as well as from France and Germany. **Roseto degli Abruzzi**, is a nice beach with a harbor built with tourists in mind. Finally, in the south of Abruzzo, other resorts such as **Ortona**, **Fossacesia**, **Torino di Sangro**, **Casalbordino** and **San Salvo** dot the coastline. Another enticing aspect of the multitude of beaches is that they are not overrun by tourism, thus allowing the visitors to enjoy their experience even more.

CHAPTER 5

Tourism—Ski Resorts/
Mountain Activities Of Abruzzo

Abruzzo offers not only warm weather fun, but also an abundance of winter sport excitement. There are known to be at least 22 winter-related resorts with at least 368 kilometer (230 miles) of ski runs in the mountains of Abruzzo—all within a few hours of Rome. Located in the highest region of the Apennines, these ski areas are at heights nearly comparable to many Alpine resorts. Because of their proximity to the *Adriatic* and winter precipitation patterns, they often have more snow than the Alps. The resorts of Abruzzo give snow-lovers the opportunity for downhill skiing, alpine skiing, cross country skiing and snowboarding, as well as a number of other snow and winter-related activities. The most developed resort is **Roccaraso**, followed by **Campo Felice**.

Most of the ski resorts can be found in the L'Aquila province, but the Gran Sasso and the Majella offer similar resorts on the Teramo side. The largest ski area in all of central and southern Italy is located in Abruzzo. Off of the Lake of Scanno, and near the National Park of Abruzzo, is the resort of **Comprensorio dell'Alto Sangro**. This large resort is renowned in the Italian ski circuits and has been the site of national ski championships. This resort is so large that it covers three communes or municipalities, Rivisondoli, Pesvovostanzo and Roccaraso (known as "the triangle"). It's known for having elegant boutiques to go along with its winter and sports facilities. Near-by are the ski resorts of **Passo Godi** and **Monte Rotondo**, which have everything from hotels to ski schools and campsites.

In the National Park of Abruzzo there is an excellent and elegant resort called **Pescaseroli.** This resort has its share of hotels, campsites and skiing schools and also boasts of a National History Museum. In the nearby locality of Macchiavana, there is another small resort called **Opi**, which is known for its cross country skiing, along with hotels and a ski school. One of the most modern and advanced ski resorts in the Apennine Mountains of Abruzzo is **Campo Felice**. This resort has the amenities of restaurants and bars right on the ski runs (no need to remove your skis) and one of the best artificial snow-making systems (with a number of snow cannons) in central Italy. Hotels, ski schools and rentable apartments are all in the vicinity, which is typically deemed to be between the municipalities of Rocca di Cambio and Rocca di Mezzo. If you would like to stay in the area for more skiing, the small resorts of **Gambarale** and **Pizzoferrato** are also near-by.

If you would like the unique experience to ski while overlooking the Adriatic Sea, there is the **Passo Lanciano-Majelletta** resort. This resort is about an hour from Pescara and Chieti and considered to have excellent amenities. In the same vicinity is **Ovindoli-Magnola** and its top-of-the-line facilities from ski related activities to night clubs. The resorts of **Marsia** and **Cappadocia Camporotondo** sit on the border of Abruzzo and Lazio (the same province where Rome is located). These resorts, with hotels, campsites and ski schools, would be the best choices if you were on your way to or from the Italian capital. Near Teramo, there are the resorts of **Prati di Tivo**, which sits at the "Tetto d'Abruzzo" or the "Roof of Abruzzo" and **Prato Selva** and **Monte Piselli**. All of these resorts have their share of ski runs, lifts, hotels, campsites and ski schools. Other resorts in Abruzzo include **Campo di Giove**, which boasts a cableway, the near-by **Passo San Leonardo,** and finally, another well-known resort area, **Campo Imperatore**. Abruzzo also is popular for cross country skiing, especially on the high plain of Campo Imperatore in the Gran Sasso, as well as the **Piana Grande** in the Majella.

The mountain towns of Abruzzo have embraced the winter activities that generate excitement and revenue and certainly welcome snow-lovers with a plethora of ski, snow and winter entertainment.

Mountain Activities

The mountains of Abruzzo also provide opportunities for mountain climbing and hiking. **Corno Grande** and its neighboring **Corno Piccolo**, provide a range of climbing opportunities and mountain hikes. These areas provide opportunities for both expert and novice climbers and hikers. Expert "alpinists" will find suitable sheer rock to ascend in either Corno Grande or Corno Piccolo, but you can also find other Abruzzo peaks that are off the beaten path, such as the slopes of the Majella (also suitable for climbing or hiking).

CHAPTER 6

Tourism—The National Park System of Abruzzo

The following parks lie, wholly or partially, within Abruzzo:

- Parco Nazionale d'Abruzzo, Lazio and Molise (Abruzzo National Park)
- Parco Nazionale del Gran Sasso e Monti della Laga (Gran Sasso National Park)
- Parco Nazionale della Majella (Majella National Park)
- Parco Naturale Regionale Sirente-Velino (Sirente Velino Regional Park)
- Lago di Barrea (Barrea Lake Wetlands)

One third of the region is designated as national or regional parkland.

Part of the National Park system of Italy, the **National Park of Abruzzo** (Parco Nazionale d'Abruzzo) was established on January 2, 1923. It expands to 44,000 hectares (170 square miles) and includes 22 towns and portions of the provinces of Isernia, L'Aquila and Frosinone within Abruzzo. This four season Park (Spring, Summer, Fall and Winter) is very conducive to tourism activities, which include guided tours and an abundance of nature paths. A great majority of the towns have Tour Information Centers.

The Park also has a variety of natural lakes including the Lake of Scanno, Lake of Montagna Speccata, Lake Vivo, Lake of Barrea and Lake Pantaniello. The Sangro River also has its main water source originating in the Park. The Volturno, Melfa and Giovenco Rivers also skirt the premises.

The nature paths and tours show the abundance of flora and fauna that the park has to offer. The paths wind their way through meadows of violets, forget-me-nots, peonies, irises, gentians, columbines and the famous "Our Lady's Slipper," which is a black and yellow orchid. The park is dotted with Wild Cherry, Pear and Apple trees, as well as Beech, Willows and Alders. The primary recommendation is to use the Val Fondillo and Camosciara paths, which typically begin as the Park's center.

The National Park's symbol is the Marsican Brown Bear and the Park is inhabited by a somewhat large bear population. Other wildlife known to be in the Park includes mountain goats, wolves, deer, chamois and a number of smaller mammals. The Park has been known to favor the protection and reintroduction of certain animal species, including the Marsican Brown Bear, wolves and lynx.

The Park is divided into 4 zones: Full Reserve, General Reserve, Protection Zone and Development Zone. A Center for the Apennine Ecological Studies is also present to study the various animal species.

Abruzzo is also the location of other national parks, including the **The National Park of Majella-Morrone** (*Parco Nazionale della Majella*) and **The National Park of Gran Sasso-Laga** (*Parco Nazionale del Gran Sasso e Monti della Laga*).

The National Park of Majella-Morrone was founded in 1993 and represents a park spanning the Majella mountain range and its intersection with the Morrone Mountain. The combination of these two ranges dominates the skyline of Abruzzo and can be viewed from almost all locations within its boundaries. Spanning several miles, the Park flows into the provinces of L'Aquila (the capital of Abruzzo), Pescara and Chieti.

Also established in 1993, and spanning a great number of miles, the National Park of Gran Sasso-Laga flows into the provinces of L'Aquila, Pescara, Teramo, Rieti, and Ascoli Piceno. This park system consists of the mountain chains known as Gran Sasso and Monti della Laga. This park system is home to an abundance of wildlife and that includes: wild boars, foxes, Apennine Wolf, the wild cat, chamois, peregrine falcon, buzzard, sparrow hawk, golden eagle, tree creeper, chough, wall creeper, newt, salamander and a plethora of smaller mammals.

The park also consists of the *Vomano River* and the ski resort of *Prati di Tivo*. The natural environments of both the National Park of Majella-Morrone and the National Park of Gran Sasso-Laga are amazingly beautiful with an abundance of flora and vegetation. The parks have a picturesque view for all four seasons, set against a beautiful non-changing backdrop of gorges, canyons and mountainsides.

Abruzzo is also home to 12 regional parks or natural reserves, all which were established between 1985 and 1992. These reserves are dedicated to the research of the animal species and used by students and experts in the field. The fauna of the parks and reserves include the likes of eagles, wolves, owls, falcons, hawks, wild cats and number of other species.

Abruzzo has become a well-known animal conservationist area and includes three World Wildlife Federation oasis locations (Serranella, Majella Orientale and Lago di Penne). The protected areas are environmentally important and are home to rare flora and fauna, such as the brown bear, the wolf and the chamois. These areas are part of the World Wildlife Federation-Italy system.

Most of these reserves are found in the provinces of L'Aquila, Chieti and Pescara. **Sirente Velino Regional**

Park (*Parco Naturale Regionale Sirente-Velino*) is one such regional park that is known for its underground river that creates a waterfall as it flows from nearby caves. The caves are a tourist attraction and guided tours are given to the Grotte di Stiffe by the L'Aquila Spalaeological Group. Another well-known reserve is the **Barrea Lake Wetlands** (Lago di Barrea).

CHAPTER 7

Medieval and Renaissance Towns

Abruzzo holds some of Italy's best-preserved medieval and Renaissance hill towns and that is why the region is often called the "true Italy." In the mid-20th century, Abruzzo experienced an abrupt decline in its agricultural economy and this event actually saved some of the region's most beautiful hill towns from the spread of modern development. Interestingly, many of these towns are entirely located within regional and national parks, which guarantees their continued preservation. Due to the lack of development and tourism, the most well preserved towns are said to be **Santo Stefano di Sessanio** and **Castel del Monte**, both of which lie in the Gran Sasso National Park. The lack of development and tourism in these villages now creates increased interest in the latter. The search for these once Medici ruled hill towns and the "true Italy" can be found on the edge of the high plain of Campo Imperatore and situated beneath the Apennines' highest peaks. Though these are great locations to begin or end your trip through Abuzzo, the region offers an abundance of similar villages, towns and cities.

L'Aquila—The Capital of Abruzzo

L'Aquila, the regional capital of Abruzzo, is rather well-known as an Abruzzo tourist area. It is the location of the highest fortress in all of Abruzzo, La Rocca di Calascio. This fortress not only attracts tourists, but also a number of filmmakers due to its astounding features. The imposing sixteenth-century castle and hierarchical church of Santa Maria de Collemaggio are other great attractions and reasons why tourists visit L'Aquila from all over Europe. Due to its proximity to the romantic city of Rome, traces of roman architecture are certainly visible in the buildings and monuments. The National Museum of Abruzzo, located in a 16th century historic castle, is a classic example where Roman paleontology and archaeology abound in numerous displays of art.

Other notable monuments include the Fontana delle 99 Cannelle, which is a fountain consisting of 99 spouts and the pink and white marble Basilica di Santa Maria di Collemaggio, which has a Holy Door and boasts a gothic interior. Santa Maria del Soccorso and Santa Maria Paganica are other cathedrals certainly worth visiting.

Piazza Garibaldi – Baroque Fountain – Sulmona

Sulmona

Hemmed in by mountains and sitting comfortably in a lush valley, Sulmona is a prosperous small city with a bustling, ancient core. Sulmona has various piazzas, churches and palaces of historical and tourist interest. Some of these include:

- Piazza Garibaldi is the main piazza, which includes a span of Gothic, 12th century Roman aqueducts and a large baroque era fountain at its center. This is the center of town and the square hosts a market twice a week on Wednesdays and Saturdays. The piazza is also famous for two tourist attracting events. The Maddona che Scappa in Piazza (Easter ceremony) involves a procession of a statue of the Madonna, whose bearers race across the piazza to meet the statue of the resurrected Christ. Every summer, a Palio style medieval festival and horse race, known as Giostra Cavalleresca, takes place in the piazza.
- Piazza XX Settembre, another of the main squares of the city, includes a bronze statue of the Roman poet Ovid. Ovid was born in Sulmona and many credit him with writing the first love poems and helping to create the St. Valentine's Day holiday.
- Palazzo Annunziata—A Palace containing an excellent museum depicting the Roman history of the city, as well as various artifacts.
- Cattedrale di San Panfilo is the city's primary cathedral and sits on the northwest side of the old city and was built on the site of a Roman temple. It contains a crypt which retains its Romanesque appearance despite the 18th Century renovation of the main church.
- Chiesa della St. Annuziata—A baroque church which includes a fine example of architecture, an ornate interior and bell tower.

- Corso Ovidio—The city's main thoroughfare that connects the cathedrals and the major piazzas and is also lined by elegant covered arcades, shops, cafes, and parks. The road is closed nightly to traffic, allowing for leisurely strolls by pedestrians.

The city also has several other historical palaces: Palazzo Meliorati, Palace Sanità, Palazzo Tabassi, Palace Sardi, and Palazzo Sardi. A visit to Sulmona can start through one of its ancient doors, one of which is of Roman age—Porta Romana. This ancient door will lead you towards the churches of Saint Filippo Neri and Saint Maria della Tomba in the Plebiscito Square.

Other churches certainly worth visiting include San Francesco delle Scarpe, which was constructed in the 13th century and San Panfilo, an 11th century cathedral. Much of Sulmona's heritage is based on the production of *confetti,* the sugar-coated almonds presented to guests at Italian weddings and a number of other events (also known as Jordan Almonds). There is also a small, but burgeoning jewelry industry.

This once walled city also has remnants of ruins just outside of its gates. Vestiges of an amphitheater, a theatre, and thermae exist at the foot of the Monte Morrone, as are some ruins of masonry buildings, probably belonging to a Roman villa, traditionally believed to be of Ovidio Nasone (Ovid), Italy's most famous ancient Latin poet (Amores and Metamorphoses)—circa 43 b.c. Nearby is an excellent Roman-period archaeological site, which is a temple dedicated to Ercole Curino, also known as the god Zeus. Sulmona also has a mountainside hermitage said to be Eremo di Sant'Onofrio. This location gave shelter to the only outgoing Pope of history: Celestino V, known as the "Pope of the great refusal"—cited by Dante in the Divina Commedia. Sulmona was also the home of Pope Innocenzo VII.

Chieti

Chieti, like Sulmona, sinks its origins in a mythological past and it was founded by the hero Achille, who aptly named it Teate in honor of its mother. In the war against Rome, Chieti was the capital of the ancient people of Marrucini, who were the allies of Sanniti. Subsequently, Teate Marrocinorum made an alliance with Rome and became a political center in 91 a.d.

Remnants of the Roman period still have scattered evidences in Chieti, such as the Roman Theatre, and the ancient Roman reservoir of thermal baths, Tempietti Romani.

The Cathedral of San Giustino, built by Bishop Teodorico (840 a.d.), has a variety of interesting frescoes on its interior walls and an ornate bell tower. The cathedral is specifically known for windows created by Bartolomeo di Giacomo. Other churches worth visiting include the San Giovanni of the Cappuccini and Saint Peter.

Chieti is also home to the National Archaeological Museum of Abruzzo, which has ancient Roman statutes and pieces of sculpture dating back to the pre-Roman period. In Chieti and you will also find another distinct and famous museum, the National Museum of Antiquities, which houses important art and literature from Italian and Roman culture.

Teramo

Teramo is situated between the highest mountain in the Apennine range, the Gran Sasso d'Italia, and the Adriatic coast and at the confluence of the Tordino and Vezzola

Rivers. The diversity of the city is shown in events held each year. In May, an art exhibit is the primary attraction (Maggio Festeggiante). During the summer months, the Interamnia World Cup, an international handball tournament, is held in Teramo and, in October, there is an international photography film show.

Teramo has become a larger tourist attraction destination due to its historic 11th and 13th century cathedrals and monuments. Some of the primary attractions include the remains of a Roman theater and amphitheatre, as well as 1st century b.c. ornate pavements. Other Roman era sites include the Torre Bruciata, a 2nd century b.c. tower. There are a number of churches worth viewing. Those churches include: the Cathedral of Saint Bernardo, the Romanesque church of Sant'Antonio, church of San Getulio, sanctuary of Madonna delle Grazie, church of Santa maria de Praediis and the church of San Domenico. The 14th century Palazzo Vescovile (Bishop's Palace) is another interesting site.

Lanciano

Lanciano is one of the most beautiful and oldest cities of Abruzzo. Lanciano was built-in 1087 b.c. and can be called the real Italian city, because of its unique character and features. The entire city is located in the mountains and has breath-taking scenery. Though ancient, Lanciano has modern facilities and accommodations. Lanciano has a wide variety of shops, coffee bars, hotels, restaurants, clubs, stadiums, and shopping malls.

Ortona

Ortona is another well-known seaside city in Abruzzo, famous for its history and ancient castles and is an important commercial port for all of Abruzzo. The seaside location enables tourist to travel a range of roads, which provide a picturesque view of the Adriatic Sea. Tourists in Ortona are permitted to join the fishermen on fishing expeditions.

Pacentro – View of the ancient town in the Appenine Mountains from a distance

Pacentro

Pacentro a small, medieval village features a 14th century castle, Castle of the Caldora (Cantelmo), which has two intact towers. Pacentro has not been influenced by modernization and is physically located in the National Park of the Majella (Parco Nazionale della Majella). Pacentro has several other historic sites, including the Church of San Marcello, founded in 1047, and is the most ancient of the village. The church is known for its frescoes and a wooden carved portal (1697). Other buildings of significance include the Church Madre, which has a beautiful bell tower and the noble palaces: Palazzo la Rocca, Palazzo Tonno, Palace Massa, and Palazzo Avolio. Outside from the village it is advisable to visit the Grotta di Colle Nusca, which includes rock paintings of hunting scenes painted thousands of years ago.

Raiano

Raiano sits in the province of L'Aquila and on the slopes of Mount Lo Pago. Nearby is the Salto River and the excellent Natural Reserve of the Gorges of San Venancio. An important Middle Ages location, Raiano once sat above the hill of Castellone and the Roman Catrum Radiani. Around the 25th century, the town's inhabitants decided to move the center of town downstream. The old section of Raiano is now called the district of Saint Anthony. The town sits along the ancient route between Foggia and Celano.

Interesting sites to visit include the Hermitage of San Venanzio, the Capuchin Monastery and the Clock Tower above the oldest entrance to the town. There are also several richly decorated noble palaces and mansions, as well as churches, which include: San Onofrio, Santa Maria Maggiore, Saint Andrew, Saint John, Saint Anthony, Our Lady of Contra (one of the oldest with Roman traces), Our Lady of Grace (medieval origins) and the Convent of Zoccolanti.

Scanno

Located between the upper Sagittario valley and the Parco Nazionale d'Abruzzo, Scanno is often called the "Pearl of Abruzzo." The famous Lago di Scanno (Lake Scanno) is truly one of the best sites in Abruzzo and a favorite destination for tourists. Surrounded by rugged landscape, the people of Scanno are a tourist attraction themselves. They are best known for attempting to keep the ancient traditions of the town intact. Elderly women can be seen wearing the town's traditional costume (a major tourist attraction), as are serenades and a number of ancient festivals, including: Festival Travi, Festival Pagnottelle, Glorie di San Martino, Mira del Gallo and the famous Catenaccio, which is a procession of couples in traditional costumes. Surrounded by mountains, Scanno has many nearby ski resorts, such as Passo Godi. Every November, the Festival of St. Martin is held near Passo Godi. Here, three 70 foot wooden towers are erected and lit at sunset.

Picturesque Scanno is known for a variety of locally made products, including the damous tombolo (lacework), gold filigree jewelry creations, the renowned Abruzzese jewel, crotchet work (table cloths and blankets) and hand-made dolls depicting the traditional costumes of Scanno. Scanno is also known for its pastries, such as the traditional "mastaccioli," which are made with chocolate, almonds and pre-fermented wine.

Scanno history reflects an early Roman settlement and it is depicted in the Museo della Lana (museum), which reconstructs the identity of the town. Other sites of note include the main entrance to the town, Piazza Santa Maria della Valle, and the historical center of town. The nearby town of **Villalago**, right on Lake Scanno, is also very picturesque.

San Vito

San Vito is known for it view of mountains and sea front. It is a beautifully situated sea side resort with developed beaches and frequented by tourists, many who travel there via train. Regarding public transport, in 2006, a new rail link was created between Pescara and Vasto, which passes through San Vito.

San Vito is the place for fine sand beaches, crystal clear, fish-filled waters—perfect for nature lovers and scuba diving. It is also known for its tiny bays and cliffs that dot the coast. Along the coast as far as Vasto, it is possible to admire the "trabocchi", which are old stilt-constructions suspended above the sea for fishing.

In Vallevò, just outside San Vito, there is the home of the Documentation Centre on Trabocchi, where guided tours of the Trabocchi can be arranged.

Fossacesia

Fossacesia is situated in the Gulf of Venere and the town is split, like many coastal towns, into two parts—the lido or beach resort and the original old town on a hill above the lido. Fossacesia's beach is near the rocky coast of Punta Cavaluccio, which also has its share of distinctive Trabocchi. The new Marina del Sole Harbor is approximately 2 kilometers (1.5 miles) from the Val di Sangro exit. An interesting site is the Cistercian Abbey of San Giovanni in Venere. Fossacesia is on a relatively new rail link, which was created between Pescara and Vasto.

Civitella Messer Raimondo

Civitella Messer Raimondo is a mediaeval village perched on top of a hill at the foot of the Majella and overlooking Fara San Martino. Civitella, besides having a wonderful view and a beautiful landscape, is also known for vendors that sell local products (mushrooms, cold meats (also processed), oil, meat and honey). The town is also known for its craftsmen who sculpt the famous white Majella stone.

Interesting sites in Civitella include a castle right in its town center, a Roman age mosaic floor and a number of archaeological finds. The age of the village can be documented by the discovery of writings dating back to the 12th century.

In the near vicinity of Civitella there are Lake Sant'Angelo (known for it fishing), Fara San Martino (often called Pasta Valley), Cavallone's Cave (grottos located at the end of a cable car trip), Lama Dei Peligni (picnic areas and swimming pool), and Palena (approximately 15 minutes away and the nearest ski resort).

Fara San Martino

Fara San Martino is considered one of the ancient Italian capitals of pasta production. The village is located at the foot of the eastern slope of the Majella and is physically located inside the Majella National Park, which makes it possible to see deer, bears, chamois, mountain goats and golden eagles. Fara San Martino village is known for its caves, which once were said to be a refuge for shepherds and brigands.

Casoli

Casoli sits upon a hill alongside the Aventino River, which feeds into the beautiful Lake Sant' Angelo and through nearby hills. Casoli is a medieval village which contains ancient churches, such as San Rocco and San Reparata, both built between 1417 and 1587. Another site worth visiting is a large castle and its surrounding walls. Contrasting attractions includes a nearby World Wildlife Federation natural reserve, said to contain black storks, flamingos and the great white heron.

Gessopalena

Gessopalena dates back to ancient times, namely the pre-Roman and Roman periods. A castle had a strategic position that dominated the Aventino River valley and blocked the entrance onto the Majella, thus creating an important defensive position. Numerous ruins and archaeological finds are noted in the area. Gessopalena was completely destroyed during World War II. The village preserves its history and is well known for an old tradition, which is a representation of Christ's Passion. A procession crosses the village every year on Holy Wednesday.

Roccascalegna

Roccascalegna is a small town situated high above sea level and almost directly between the mountains and the sea. Roccascalegna is known for its castle, which rises on a rock of limestone above green hills covered in an abundance of vegetation. The drive through Roccascalenga or "Fondo Valle Sangro", also known as the Sangro Valley, is well worth the trip just to admire the sight of the castle.

Palombaro

If you want a stunning view of the Avello Valley, Palombaro is the village to visit. The village boasts of a Roman origin and has several sights worth viewing. These sights include the 18th century church of St. Assunta and its impressive gothic bell tower and the San Angelo Cave, which actually contains and preserves ruins from a medieval church. Also certainly worth visiting is Feudo Ugni, a natural reserve.

Torino di Sangro

Located at the mouth of the Sangro River, Torino di Sangro is considered to have the cleanest and well organized (pebbled and sandy) beaches in the area. It is also known as one of the quietest resort areas along the Cheiti coast. Torino di Sangro is split into two parts, the beach resort and the old town, which sits on a hill above the beach.

The town boasts a natural reserve, Bitopo delle Leccette Litoranee, which also includes camp sites. The 16th century parish church of San Salvatore is a main attraction. A recent public transport rail link, created between Pescara and Vasto, passes Torino di Sangro along the coast.

Lama dei Peligni

Lama dei Peligni is located below the highest point of the Majella Mountain, also known as Monte Amaro. This is an area known as an outdoor sporting natural oasis and includes activities such as, horseback riding, bike trails, swimming pools and hiking. The Pine forests and natural springs have near-by picnic areas and, of course, the town is near the Majella National Park.

Points of interest include the church of San Nicola (twenty-sixth century), which has a number of baroque furnishings, and the religious destination known as the Grottos di Sant'Angelo. There is also Naturalistic Museum. Lama dei Peligni has also been said to have been inhabited since prehistoric times and was once a key defense location on the road to Chieti.

Bomba

Situated on a well-known lake, Bomba is a welcoming place with nightlife, entertainment, restaurants, camping area and sports facilities. It recently hosted events for the Mediterranean Games, a water sports event. The lake offers boat races, boat trips, wind surfing and a wide variety of other activities during the summer months. A tree surrounded swimming pool sits near the lake and has the surrounding mountains as an imposing backdrop.

Other Interesting Towns

There are numerous ancient and medieval towns and small cities that could be mentioned, for they all have their own unique character and beauty. To name a few others which are certainly worth at least a stop for a quick espresso (if not much, much more):

Bugnara, Sant'Eufemia a Maiella, Villetta Barrea, Tocco, Cansano, Introdacqua, Popoli, Rivisondoli, Roccacasale, Roccaraso, Villa Sant'Angelo and Villa Santa Maria.

To see a listing of all of the towns and cities of Abruzzo, please see Chapter 10.

CHAPTER 8

Festivals of Abruzzo

Porta Napoli - Sulmona - 14th century gate to the city.

January:

Fara Filiorum Petri, Abruzzo: (Farchie Festival)—Festival of St. Anthony is illuminated by giant torches.

Rivisondoli, Abruzzo: Festival of the Epiphany—Live nativity scene is reenacted by hundreds in costumes portraying the arrival of the Three Kings at the manger.

Picciano, Abruzzo: Traditional Befana Festival. (Befana is an old lady who gives gifts to good children and coal to bad ones).

February:

All across Abruzzo: "Mardi Gras"—Carnival Festivities—Pre-Ash Wednesday—Carnival Parades with costumes, floats and confetti.

March/April (Spring):

Sulmona, Abruzzo: La Madonna in Piazza. The most well-known Easter festival in all of Abruzzo and seen on national news reports worldwide, this medieval pageant depicts the Virgin Mary seeing the risen Jesus—(on Easter Sunday).

San Valentino, Abruzzo: Frittata or giant omelet Festival (on Good Friday).

L'Aquila, Abruzzo: Good Friday Procession. (At sunset on Good Friday.)

Gessopelena, Abruzzo: The village preserves an old tradition: the representation of Christ's Passion, it plays every Holy Wednesday and the procession crosses the entirety of the old village.

All across Abruzzo: Easter parades and festivities taking place during the day and at night.

May:

Bucchianico, Abruzzo: Flower Festival. This is a re-enactment of a 13th-century event concerning a military strategy that salvaged the town from destruction. This festival features costumed parades, carts covered in flowers and exquisite miniature flower floats worn on the local ladies' heads (on the third Sunday of May).

Rocca di Mezzo, Abruzzo: Daffodil Festival. Folklore dances, presentations and a parade of flowery floats celebrating the arrival of spring (on the last Sunday in May).

Cocullo, Abruzzo: Snake Handlers' Procession. A statue of the town's patron saint, St. Dominic (covered with live serpents), is carried through the town (on the first Thursday in May).

June:

Raiano, Abruzzo: Cherry Festival—A cherry tasting festival featuring cherries of all types from all over Italy.

Loreto Aprutino, Abruzzo: Procession of the Ox. This beautifully-costumed procession culminates in an ornate ox kneeling before the statue of St. Zopito (on the Monday after Pentecost).

Pianella, Abruzzo: Town Festival—A festival featuring products from the local area. Taste the local wines, cheeses and olive oil, as well as other products.

Pescara, Abruzzo: Flower Festival—A festival in appreciation of flowers.

July:

Pescara, Abruzzo: Jazz Festival—Jazz music festival.

Acciano, Abruzzo: Wine and Truffle Festival. Wine from the region and the world-famous, locally-grown truffles.

Manopello, Abruzzo: Pasta Festival—A true Italian pasta-fest

San Omero, Abruzzo: Beer Festival—Many brands and types of beer are available for tasting and there is a large variety of locally—grown produce for the same purpose.

Villamagna, Abruzzo: Historical re-enactment of the Turks and St. Margarita event.

August:

Sulmona, Abruzzo: A Palio style medieval festival and horse race, known as Giostra Cavalleresca, takes place in the piazza.

Cappelle Sul Tavo, Abruzzo: Palio del Pupo—Costumed races. The festival also includes wine, cheese and olive oil tasting, as well as other local products.

Cappelle Sul Tavo, Abruzzo: Palio of the Puppets—Giant puppets form a procession through the town—a large fireworks display ends the festival.

Cappelle Sul Tavo, Abruzzo: Ploughing Festival—Re-enactment of a 17th-century custom, culminating in a race to plough the most perfect lined-indentation or seam (on the last Saturday in August). Local wines, cheese, olive oil, as well as other local products are often judged and tasted.

Popoli, Abruzzo: Trout and Shrimp Festival—A seafood festival.

Celano, Abruzzo: Costumed procession and fireworks are part of the festivities (in late August).

Cepagatti, Abruzzo: Historical parade with floats, fireworks and a number of other festivities. Included is a traditional wedding ceremony, which re-enactments a unique local wedding custom.

Collicello di Cagnano, Abruzzo: Wild Boar Festival—Includes the tasting of their famous Wild Boar sausages and other products made from wild boar. Taste the local wines, cheese, olive oil, as well as other local products.

Pescara, Abruzzo: Festival of the Fishermen—Seafood festival held on the first Sunday in August—Includes a procession in the sea.

September:

Lanciano, Abruzzo: Medieval pageant with the main event being a horse race. Taste the local wines, cheeses, olive oil, as well as other local products.

Pacentro, Abruzzo: Festival of the Madonna of Loreto—A traditional bare-foot "gypsy race" down the mountainside (on the first Sunday in September).

October:

Montonico, Abruzzo: Bisenti Festa of Grapes and Wine—The local vineyards participate in a free wine-tasting festival.

Villa Santa Maria, Abruzzo: Culinary Festival—A true culinary event, which attract world-famous chefs who originate from the region. The three-day festival allows them to demonstrate their skills, techniques and recipes that date back over centuries. You can also taste the local wines, cheese and olive oil, as well as other products.

November:

Scanno, Abruzzo: Bonfire Festival—Enormous bonfires are lit on the surrounding hillsides to commemorate the Festival of St. Martin.

Valle Castellana, Abruzzo: Chestnut and Potato Festival—Two local products are featured.

December:

Carunchio, Abruzzo: White Truffle Festival—Taste the local white truffles, local wines, cheeses, olive oil and other products.

All across Abruzzo—Towns, villages and cities depict nativity scenes in town squares (piazza) and churches and conduct a variety of processions and religious festivals to celebrate Christmas.

CHAPTER 9

The Food of Abruzzo

The Abruzzo region, has an abundance of sheep farming and agriculture throughout the region and those products are used to create some of the most traditional meals in all of Italy. The Abruzzese cuisine is simple, delicious and made with genuine Italian ingredients. From the golden Abruzzo olive oil to the high quality Abruzzo truffles, a palate of pleasing dishes is always available. Abruzzo food is generally very simple and inexpensive, but still delicious. During times of celebration, the cooks of Abruzzo become more elaborate. A great example of this is the 50 course feast of the Panarda.

The mountains in Abruzzo are also full of small and ancient towns that have a very unique, but also a simple gastronomy characterized by different basic ingredients. The cuisines of Abruzzo are divided into basically two parts: the mountains and the sea.

Pasta Region

Abruzzo is home to one of the Italian capitals of pasta production, namely Fara San Martino, which is a small town at the foot of the Majella. Since ancient times there have been three specialized manufacturers that now export all over the world. These manufacturers include: Pastificio Cavalier Cocco, Pastificio De Cecco, and Pastificio Del Verde.

The region is also famous for its pasta production, in particular what is known as *maccheroni alla chitarra* (loosely translated as *Guitar String Pasta*). This particular recipe has become, in fact, a symbol for the whole region. The name comes from the fact that maccheroni are prepared using a real string instrument consisting of a rectangular wooden frame on which are fixed some very thin steel strings—resembling guitar strings. Abruzzo is famous for its excellent dried pasta, the best of which is made by local artisans.

This traditional first-course Abruzzo pasta is often covered with marinara sauce made from locally grown tomatoes or the ever classic tomatoes with basil sauce. Due to the abundance of sheep, you will also find another traditional sauce that accompany this kind of maccheroni, namely lamb ragù.

Maccheroni alla Chitarra

Maccheroni are squared spaghetti-like noodles made from fresh pasta dough. The pasta is often served with a traditional lamb ragu cooked in a *catturo*, or copper pan, with onions and diavolillo, the famously hot, dried chili pepper.

The Abruzzo Table

The meats include locally made sausage and farm raised pork, lamb, duck and goose. Breeding is a main activity in Abruzzo, which makes the meat the most important ingredient in all of the regional recipes. One of the most well-known dishes of Abruzzo is lamb-based and it is called Icaporchiato lamb. Icaporchiato basically refers to lamb boiled in water and contains little to no flavoring, but still produces a tasteful dish. This system of cooking is said to have originated when shepherds had little opportunity to cook lamb, and when they did they needed a quick means of preparation. Lamb is also often prepared using a recipe called *Cacio e uova*, meaning with pecorino cheese and egg. There is also Arrosticini, which are thin mutton skewers grilled over charcoal (baby kebabs). Lamb is very famous in the mountains and thus is the dominant dish there. It has consequently overtaken mutton and is kept reserved for special occasions like Easter, marriages or baptisms.

Pork is another widely used traditional meat dish in Abruzzo. The processing of pork, another widespread activity in the region, has lead to the creation of a great selection of hams, sausages, and salamis. One popular selection is the traditional liver sausage, which is often preserved in oil. Other traditional products include: Soppressate, smoked ham, mortadella from the Campotosto area and ventricina, produced near Chieti, though many believe those from Teramo are the best. Ventricina is a pork sausage found in both Abruzzo and near-by Molise and stuffed into a casing made from pork stomach, as opposed to intestine. One of the more well-known pork dishes is often called *'ndocaa 'ndocca*, which is a stew of boiled pork meat.

Fish and Seafood Dishes

The fish and seafood dishes are usually more elaborate than their meat counterparts. The coastal cooking is obviously more rich of fish-dishes, and some of the more well-know are fish-soups from coastal towns such as Pescara, Vasto and San Vito. These dishes are better known as *brodetti*. Overall, the recipes tend to rely less on tomato and more on pepperoncino, especially in the fish stews. The other main Abruzzo seafood meals encompass great mussels, shellfish, bluefish and rock fish and are typically served with pasta, risotto, salad and soups. Other coastal fish dishes of note include cod, sole, anchovies, prawns and cuttlefish.

Cheeses

What would an Italian meal be without some form of cheese? Sheep farming is the most common form of animal farming in Abruzzo, which explains its importance in the role of regional gastronomy. Sheep's milk cheeses dominate Abruzzo's dairy production.

The cheese from Abruzzo farms, such as Burrelle (butter filled), Caciocavallo (a bigger form of dried mozzarella), Caciottta (cow's and sheep's milk) and Scamorza (dried mozzarella—young and aged) from the area of Rivisondoli and Pescocostanzo, are known to be excellent. There is also Pecorino (ewe's milk cheese, either fresh or seasoned) and sheep ricotta, as well as excellent dairy products, such as trecce (platted), bocconcini (very small fresh mozzarella), and fiordilatte (small fresh mozzarella) all produced in the region.

From the Farm

Truffles are a high quality product of the Abruzzo region and a great source of pride to its citizens. Amazingly, there are 28 truffle varieties in Abruzzo. The black truffle (tartufo nero) is the best known and most widely used. Many dishes, in particular, white sauces used on pasta, are heavily influenced by the truffle. Truffles are typically found by the locals and their truffle-sniffing dog, though pigs are sometimes also used. The delicacy is a prominent industry in the region.

Another typical ingredient of this zone is the red garlic of Sulmona. This garlic is covered in a wine red skin with white cloves and is larger than normal in size. Just before harvesting, the garlic is more floral, often referred to as producing the "*zolla.*"

Other interesting products grown in Abruzzo include lentils, grass peas and a large selection of farm fresh vegetables.

As with any excellent meal, the spices play a large role. One such prominent Abruzzo spice is saffron. Saffron comes from the tiny Crocus flower, which blooms in late winter to early spring. The Province of L'Aquila produces excellent saffron. The L'Aquila saffron is so highly regarded that it is shipped across the world and it is one of the few places in the world where it is farmed.

Abruzzo is also a big producer of extra virgin olive oil and the region has three classified varieties. The extra-virgin olive oil of Abruzzo is just as good as any of the best Italian oils. Though it is a very important commercial industry in the area, much production still comes from family-operated businesses. During November and December, families are also known to spend weekends picking their olives and taking them to the local mill press for personal olive oil production.

Fresh fruit finishes off a healthy meal. Many types of fruit are grown in Abruzzo, including cherries, walnuts, figs, strawberries, plums, and, of course, grapes. The most famous of the grape varieties are the Montepulciano grapes, which are small, black grapes that are made into the prestigious Montepulciano d'Abruzzo wine.

Bee keepers produce excellent and delicious tasting honey all across Abruzzo. The royal jelly and propoli honeys are considered superb.

Dessert

For dessert, the famous pizzelles (wafers/waffles) are the major draw, but so are bocconotti (small pastry—nut filled with dried fruit and cocoa—best known from Castel Frentano). The traditional Biscotti are always available, as are the Torrones (soft nougat candy) and the world-famous Abruzzo (Sulmona) Confetti (sugared almonds). Sulmona is considered the world-capital of *confetti*, also known as Jordan or sugared almonds. The other types of confetti are filled with liquor and jellies. Other traditional sweet pastries of Abruzzo are mostaccioli (chocolate covered nut biscuit), and cicerchiata (pastry balls stuck together with honey).

Wines/Beverages

Abruzzo is also known as a good region for grape growing. Abruzzo is considered to be the fifth largest producer of wine globally and has Italy's highest average yield for bulk wines (at 110 million gallons)—per various sources. Since it is mostly a mountainous and hilly region, it is perfect for growing grapevines with the most common grapes grown in the region being Montepulciano and Trebbiano, though the wineries are working to produce more varieties.

The Montepulciano and Tebbiano grapes produce excellent soft red wines with full, rich and robust flavors. Abruzzo is primarily known for the red Montepulciano d'Abruzzo variety. This robust and strong wine is also produced in the Montelpulciano d'Abruzzo Colline Teramane variety. Montepulciano wines brands that have been found abroad include Dragani and Citra. The other primary produced wines of the region are Trebbiano d'Abruzzo (red), Trebbiano d'Abruzzo (white), Contro Guerra and the red Cerasuolo. All of these wines are excellent and beginning to obtain international recognition. The wines of the region are ideally suitable with red meat and aged cheeses.

The many Abruzzo-made liqueurs include chocolate, coffee, cherry, strawberry and blueberry. The Pescara area is most famous for liqueurs such as, Centerba (100 grasses), which has a unique taste and a vivid green color and Aurum, which is an orange flavored liquor. Many of these beverages are over 40 percent proof or have even a higher alcohol content.

CHAPTER 10

Economy

and

Demographics

Abruzzo had seen steady economic growth since the end of World War II, primarily from the 1950's. An example of this would be the growth in per capita income or Gross Domestic Product (GDP) percentages, when compared to that of the wealthiest regions in northern Italy:

- 195-53%
- 1971-65%
- 1994-76%
- 2003-84%

Today, the per capita income and Gross Domestic Product of Abruzzo exceeds 84%, surpassing the growth rate of every other region in Italy or "Mezziogiorno." Abruzzo has also attained higher education and productivity growth, per capita, than the rest of the country.

Much of the growth can be attributed to the construction of superhighways that opened up the isolated and mountainous Abruzzo region to the rest of Italy and Europe. Highways constructed from Rome to Pescara and Rome to Teramo were major catalysts in opening up the region to investment. Abruzzo's transportation equipment, telecommunications and mechanical engineering industrial sectors were great beneficiaries of expansion, due to the construction of the superhighway systems.

Demographics

Regional accents of Abruzzo include Teramano, Abruzzese Orientale Adriatico and Abruzzese Occidentale. The first two form a portion of the *Italiano meridionale-interno* dialect, primarily of southern Italy and also known simply as "Neapolitan." This can be attributed to the region having been part of the Kingdom of Naples and the Two Sicilies, while the Italian of the L'Aquila Province is related to the Osco-Umbro dialect, more so of central Italy, which includes that of Rome. Though an Abruzzo dialect exists, it is not necessarily that prevalent or different than other areas of Italy. One of the more prestigious universities of the United States, Harvard University, actually bases an intensive summer language program in the resort town of Vasto, which is located on Abruzzo's Adriatic coast.

From the early to mid-20th century Abruzzo's population was in decline, primarily due to economic conditions in Europe related to the two world wars. Many Italians, including a number of Abruzzesi, left the country and immigrated to North America, South America and Australia.

It wasn't until the 1970's that the population trend began to reverse. Today, the current population of Abruzzo is estimated to approximately 1,400,000. The four provinces of Abruzzo, Pescara, Chieti, L'Aquila and Teramo, all have populations in the 300,000 to 400,000 range. Chieti has the largest population of the provinces, followed by Pescara, L'Aquila and Teramo. The population is split almost evenly amongst males and females.

There are 305 municipalities in the four provinces of Abruzzo. The ten with the largest populations are:

1	**Pescara**
2	**L'Aquila**
3	**Teramo**
4	**Chieti**
5	**Montesilvano**

6	**Avezzano**
7	**Vasto**
8	**Lanciano**
9	**Sulmona**
10	**Roseto degli Abruzzi**

"Settembre, andiamo. E' tempo di migrare.
Ora in terra d'Abruzzi i miei pastori
Lascian gli stazzi e vanno verso il mar . . . ."

"September, let's go. It's time to migrate.
Now in Abruzzo my shepherds leave the folds
and go toward the sea."

Gabriele D'Annunzio emblematically summarizes the importance of sheep farming in Abruzzo in this well-know phrase. The region of Abruzzo was well known for what is called the *transumanza*, which is the migratory movement of sheep during the winter months to southern locations, primarily the region of Puglia.

Cities and Towns of Abruzzo—
Alphabetical Order

<u>A</u>

- Abbateggio
- Acciano
- Aielli
- Alanno
- Alba Adriatica
- Alfedena
- Altino, Abruzzo
- Ancarano
- Anversa degli Abruzzi
- Archi, Abruzzo
- Ari, Abruzzo
- Arielli
- Arsita
- Ateleta
- Atessa
- Atri, Abruzzo
- Avezzano

<u>B</u>

- Balsorano
- Barete
- Barisciano
- Barrea
- Basciano
- Bellante
- Bisegna
- Bisenti
- Bolognano

- <u>Bomba, Abruzzo</u>
- <u>Borrello</u>
- <u>Brittoli</u>
- <u>Bucchianico</u>
- <u>Bugnara</u>
- <u>Bussi sul Tirino</u>

<u>C</u>

- <u>Cagnano Amiterno</u>
- <u>Calascio</u>
- <u>Campli</u>
- <u>Campo di Giove</u>
- <u>Campotosto</u>
- <u>Canistro</u>
- <u>Canosa Sannita</u>
- <u>Cansano</u>
- <u>Canzano</u>
- <u>Capestrano</u>
- <u>Capistrello</u>
- <u>Capitignano</u>
- <u>Caporciano</u>
- <u>Cappadocia, Abruzzo</u>
- <u>Cappelle sul Tavo</u>
- <u>Caramanico Terme</u>
- <u>Carapelle Calvisio</u>
- <u>Carpineto della Nora</u>
- <u>Carpineto Sinello</u>
- <u>Carsoli</u>
- <u>Carunchio</u>
- <u>Casacanditella</u>
- <u>Casalanguida</u>
- <u>Casalbordino</u>
- <u>Casalincontrada</u>

- Casoli
- Castel Castagna
- Castel del Monte, Abruzzo
- Castel di Ieri
- Castel di Sangro
- Castel Frentano
- Castelguidone
- Castellafiume
- Castellalto
- Castelli, Abruzzo
- Castelvecchio Calvisio
- Castelvecchio Subequo
- Castiglione a Casauria
- Castiglione Messer Marino
- Castiglione Messer Raimondo
- Castilenti
- Catignano
- Celano
- Celenza sul Trigno
- Cellino Attanasio
- Cepagatti
- Cerchio
- Cermignano
- Chieti
- Città Sant'Angelo
- Civita d'Antino
- Civitaluparella
- Civitaquana
- Civitella Alfedena
- Civitella Casanova
- Civitella del Tronto
- Civitella Messer Raimondo
- Civitella Roveto

- <u>Cocullo</u>
- <u>Collarmele</u>
- <u>Collecorvino</u>
- <u>Colledara</u>
- <u>Colledimacine</u>
- <u>Colledimezzo</u>
- <u>Collelongo</u>
- <u>Collepietro</u>
- <u>Colonnella</u>
- <u>Comuni of the Province of Chieti</u>
- <u>Comuni of the Province of Teramo</u>
- <u>Controguerra</u>
- <u>Corfinio</u>
- <u>Corropoli</u>
- <u>Cortino</u>
- <u>Corvara, Abruzzo</u>
- <u>Crecchio</u>
- <u>Crognaleto</u>
- <u>Cugnoli</u>
- <u>Cupello</u>

<u>D</u>
- <u>Dogliola</u>

<u>E</u>
- <u>Elice</u>

<u>F</u>
- <u>Fagnano Alto</u>
- <u>Fallo</u>
- <u>Fano Adriano</u>
- <u>Fara Filiorum Petri</u>
- <u>Fara San Martino</u>

- Farindola
- Filetto
- Fontecchio
- Fossa, Abruzzo
- Fossacesia
- Fraine
- Francavilla al Mare
- Fresagrandinaria
- Frisa
- Frondarola
- Furci

G

- Gagliano Aterno
- Gamberale
- Garrano Basso
- Gessopalena
- Gioia dei Marsi
- Gissi
- Giuliano Teatino
- Giulianova
- Goriano Sicoli
- Guardiagrele
- Guilmi

I

- Introdacqua
- Isola del Gran Sasso d'Italia

L

- L'Aquila
- Lama dei Peligni
- Lanciano

- <u>Lecce nei Marsi</u>
- <u>Lentella</u>
- <u>Lettomanoppello</u>
- <u>Lettopalena</u>
- <u>Liscia</u>
- <u>Loreto Aprutino</u>
- <u>Luco dei Marsi</u>
- <u>Lucoli</u>

<u>M</u>

- <u>Magliano (Torricella Sicura)</u>
- <u>Magliano de' Marsi</u>
- <u>Manoppello</u>
- <u>Martinsicuro</u>
- <u>Massa d'Albe</u>
- <u>Miglianico</u>
- <u>Molina Aterno</u>
- <u>Montazzoli</u>
- <u>Montebello di Bertona</u>
- <u>Montebello sul Sangro</u>
- <u>Monteferrante</u>
- <u>Montefino</u>
- <u>Montelapiano</u>
- <u>Montenerodomo</u>
- <u>Monteodorisio</u>
- <u>Montereale, Abruzzo</u>
- <u>Montesilvano</u>
- <u>Monticelli (Teramo)</u>
- <u>Montorio al Vomano</u>
- <u>Morino</u>
- <u>Morro d'Oro</u>
- <u>Mosciano Sant'Angelo</u>
- <u>Moscufo</u>

- Mozzagrogna

N

- Navelli
- Nereto
- Nocciano
- Notaresco

O

- Ocre
- Ofena
- Opi, Abruzzo
- Oricola
- Orsogna
- Ortona
- Ortona dei Marsi
- Ortucchio
- Ovindoli

P

- Pacentro
- Padula (Cortino)
- Paganica
- Paglieta
- Palena, Abruzzo
- Palmoli
- Palombaro
- Penna Sant'Andrea
- Pennadomo

P

- Pennapiedimonte
- Penne, Abruzzo

- Perano
- Pereto
- Pescara
- Pescasseroli
- Pescina
- Pescocostanzo
- Pescosansonesco
- Pettorano sul Gizio
- Piane di Collevecchio
- Pianella
- Picciano
- Pietracamela
- Pietraferrazzana
- Pietranico
- Pineto
- Pizzoferrato
- Pizzoli
- Poggio Picenze
- Poggiofiorito
- Pollutri
- Popoli
- Prata d'Ansidonia
- Pratola Peligna
- Pretoro
- Prezza, Abruzzo

Q

- Quadri

R

- Raiano
- Rapino
- Ripa Teatina

- Rivisondoli
- Rocca di Botte
- Rocca di Cambio
- Rocca di Mezzo
- Rocca Pia
- Rocca San Giovanni
- Rocca Santa Maria
- Roccacasale
- Roccamontepiano
- Roccamorice
- Roccaraso
- Roccascalegna
- Roccaspinalveti
- Roio del Sangro
- Rosciano
- Rosello
- Roseto degli Abruzzi

S

- Salle, Abruzzo
- San Benedetto dei Marsi
- San Benedetto in Perillis
- San Buono
- San Demetrio ne' Vestini
- San Giovanni Lipioni
- San Giovanni Teatino
- San Martino sulla Marrucina
- San Pio delle Camere
- San Salvo
- San Valentino in Abruzzo Citeriore
- San Vincenzo Valle Roveto
- San Vito Chietino
- Sant'Egidio alla Vibrata

- Sant'Eufemia a Maiella
- Sant'Eusanio del Sangro
- Sant'Eusanio Forconese
- Sant'Omero
- Santa Maria Imbaro
- Sante Marie
- Santo Stefano di Sessanio
- Scafa
- Scanno, Abruzzo
- Scerni
- Schiavi di Abruzzo
- Scontrone
- Scoppito
- Scurcola Marsicana
- Secinaro
- Serramonacesca
- Silvi
- Spiano
- Spoltore
- Sulmona

T

- Tagliacozzo
- Taranta Peligna
- Teramo
- Tione degli Abruzzi
- Tocco da Casauria
- Tofo Sant'Eleuterio
- Tollo
- Torano Nuovo
- Torino di Sangro
- Tornareccio
- Tornimparte

- Torre de' Passeri
- Torrebruna
- Torrevecchia Teatina
- Torricella Peligna
- Torricella Sicura
- Tossicia
- Trasacco
- Treglio
- Tufillo
- Turrivalignani

V

- Vacri
- Valle Castellana
- Valle Pezzata
- Valva (city)
- Vasto
- Vicoli
- Villa Celiera
- Villa Sant'Angelo
- Villa Santa Lucia degli Abruzzi
- Villa Santa Maria
- Villalago
- Villalfonsina
- Villamagna
- Villavallelonga
- Villetta Barrea
- Vittorito

CHAPTER 11

History

It is said that humans have inhabited Abruzzo since Neolithic times with an approximation of 6,500 b.c. The name Abruzzo appears to derive from the Middle Ages and the Latin "Aprutium," or the Latin expression "a Bruttiis" (from the Bruttii), interpreted as stating that the first inhabitants were the Bruzi people, who moved south to occupy Calabria or the Latin "aper" (boar)—inferring that Aprutium was the "land of boars" or from "abruptum" (steep and rugged land). This area of Italy was already inhabited in pre-Roman times by the pre-Indo-European culture of the Piceni and subsequently by various Italic tribes.

During the Roman era, the region was known as Flaminia et Picenum, Picenum, Sabina et Samnium, and/or Campania et Samnium and the inhabitants were honored by Caesar as citizens of Rome. The City of Corfinio—current village of Pentima—is located within the province (known as Corfinuim in ancient Italy) and it was the primary city of those called the "Paeligni." The name Italia was imposed upon the Roman Republic by the conquering Italic tribes of the contemporary Abruzzo region, centering in the area of Corfinium (Corfinio). Entering Corfinio from the east, a plaque can be observed commemorating and attributing the designation of the adopted name "Italia" to the peninsula by the Italic people of the region. After the fall of the Western Roman Empire and the Lombard invasions, "Italy" or "Italian" gradually became the collective name for diverse states appearing on the peninsula and holdings overseas.

During the 12th century, the emperor Frederick the First named the region *Listitieratu Aprutii* and made it part of the Kingdom of Southern Italy, which maintained its own identity until 1860 despite its share of turmoil. L'Aquila, the current regional capital, was probably founded in 1254 to sustain an anti-imperial uprising in the western part of the region.

The Kingdom of Southern Italy passed from Spain to Austria and, in 1735, became the property of the French Bourbons. When Napoleon assumed power, his brother-in-law Joachim Murat became the king of Southern Italy. The poet Gabriele Rossetti from Vasto was appointed Secretary of Public Education in the administration of the kingdom. Rossetti later lived in exile in London, where his son, Dante Gabriel Rossetti, became a well-known painter and was one of the founders of the pre-Raphaelite movement. The Kingdom of Southern Italy came to an end in 1860 following Garibaldi's victorious campaign that united modern Italy. Abruzzo was then joined with Molise into a single region known as "Abruzzi" or "Abruzzi e Molise." The term *Abruzzi* derives from the time when the region was part of the Kingdom of the Two Sicilies, which had its capital in Naples.

Until 1963, Abruzzo was known as "Abruzz"—which included the current regions of Abruzzo and Molise.

The Italian government continued and expanded civil works started by the Bourbons, such as draining the Lake Fucino creating 140 square kilometers of excellent agricultural land. In addition, new railways and highways were built. In 1923, the National Park of Abruzzi was established protecting an area of 400 square kilometers as a local habitat sanctuary. During the 1970's and 1980's the Adriatic coast saw the birth of a new industry-based economy which, along with tourism, provided a much needed stable economy for the local population.

CHAPTER 12

Travel Information

Airports

The Abruzzo International Airport is located in Pescara. It is currently the only airport that accepts commercial passenger flights. The airport has been known to have direct flights originating from locations within the United States. Other more regional airports do exist within Abruzzo.

Sea Ports

- The primary sea ports within Abruzzo consist of:
- Port of Pescara
- Port of Ortona
- Port of Vasto
- Port of Giulianova

Over the years, the Port of Pescara has become one of the most important ports of Italy and the Adriatic Sea. It has been honored with the Blue Flag of the European Union for the quality of services offered.

Rail Services

Existing railway lines:

- **Ferrovia Adriatica** (through the whole of Italy from north to south, along the Adriatic Sea)
- **Train Rome—Sulmona—Pescara**: Pescara-Rome railway line is along the railway line Bologna-Bari on the Adriatic. The line is important because through the Tyrrhenian coast, passing through the provinces of Pescara, Chieti and L'Aquila and ends the path to Roma Tiburtina station.

- **Sulmona—Carpinone:** The infrastructure in question is a continuation to the south of Terni-Sulmona, as part of the intermediate cross-Pescara Naples.
- **Sulmona—Terni:** Connects the regions of Umbria, Lazio and Abruzzo, Molise and then along the line-Carpinone Sulmona. (see above)
- **Avezzano railroad—Roccasecca:** Starts on the track in the town of Avezzano, and ends its journey in the town of Roccasecca, which marks the end of Lazio and the entry in the Campania region towards Cassino.
- **Giulianova—Teramo—**Connection between Teramo and Giulianova
- **Sangritana (Lanciano—Castel di Sangro):** Ties Abruzzo between the Tyrrhenian and Adriatic Seas.

Distances Between Abruzzo and Other Italian Cities

The following distances are from the "heart" or "central" Abruzzo to other cities around Italy (in miles):

- Rome—70
- Naples—154
- Florence—200
- Bologna—261
- Genoa—341
- Venice—351
- Milan—390
- Turin—447

RECIPES
OF
ABRUZZO

Having the year-round taste of Abruzzo cuisine in your household is almost as enjoyable as being there. Here are some traditional Abruzzo recipes, which will ensure that the *taste* of Abruzzo is always with you.

From soup to appetizer, main dishes to desserts, spend some time in your Abruzzo kitchen creating these delicious meals. Adding a little Multipiciano d'Abruzzo wine, such as Citra or Dragani, and some confetti (Jordan Almonds) will round out the meal. Don't forget the espresso . . . maybe with a touch of Anisette liquor. Buon Appetito!

Minestrone (Soup)

- 1 lb. tubettini pasta
- 4 potatoes (diced)
- 1 can of white or red beans
- 1 cup of celery (diced)
- 1 large can of chicken soup
- 1 cup of pasta sauce
- 1 cup of Romano cheese
- Salt/pepper

- Add chicken soup, pasta sauce, potatoes, celery and salt/pepper to pot.
- Allow potatoes to cook
- Add pasta and beans and allow pasta to cook
- Add cheese and serve

Zucchini Puffs (Appetizer)

- 3 grated zucchini
- 3 eggs
- 2 cups of flour
- ½ cup Romano cheese
- ½ cup of bread crumbs
- 2 tsp of baking powder
- Salt/pepper/parsley/garlic to taste

- Mix ingredients and drop teaspoonful size pieces into hot oil
- Cook/remove and serve

Abruzzo Chicken (Pollo)

- 2 lbs. diced, boneless chicken breasts
- 8 Pieces of cleaned garlic
- Olive oil, balsamic vinegar, salt, pepper

- Add olive oil and garlic to frying pan
- Sautee until garlic is golden
- Add chicken and salt/pepper to taste
- Sautee chicken until golden
- Add half-cup of balsamic vinegar
- Sautee until chicken is cooked

Gnocchi

- 4 lbs of peeled potatoes
- 3 lbs of flour
- 3 lbs of semolina
- 3 eggs
- 4 tbsp of salt
- Makes 8 pounds of gnocchi

- Boil potatoes—then mash—allow to cool
- Add flour, eggs, semolina, salt
- Mix and create ball of dough
- Roll dough into one/two inch strips
- Cut strips into one inch pieces
- Boil water/add salt
- Add gnocchi pieces
- Boil for 10 minutes
- Drain—add sauce and cheese

Lasagna (Pasta)

- 1 lb box of lasagna pasta
- 2 lbs of ground meat
- 1 lb of shredded Mozzarella cheese
- 1 lb Parmigianino cheese (shredded)
- 1 ½ quarts of pasta sauce
- Salt and Pepper
- Makes 1 pan of lasagna

- Sautee meat until golden—add salt/pepper to taste
- Cook pasta until tender (or directions)—add salt to water
- Place sauce at bottom of pan
- Place strips of lasagna pasta at bottom of pan
- Add meat over pasta
- Add cheese over meat
- Add sauce over cheese
- Repeat the pasta/meat/cheese/sauce (3 layers)
- Dough as top layer—add cheese and sauce over top
- Place in over for 1 hour at 400 degrees
- Let stand for five/seven minutes and serve

Biscotti (Dessert)

- 4 eggs
- 1 Tsp of almond extract
- 1 Tbsp of vanilla
- 1 cup of milk
- ½ cup of Crisco or similar
- 1/3 cup of vegetable oil
- 1 ½ cup of sugar
- 5 cups of flour
- 4 Tbsp baking powder

- Melt Crisco/grease and allow to cool
- Beat eggs/sugar together
- Add milk/vanilla/almond extract/oil and cooled grease
- Add flour and make dough
- Make two-inch wide—one-wide loaves
- Place on baking pan
- Beat one egg and brush on loaves
- Bake at 350 degrees for 45 minutes to an hour
- Remove, allow to cool and slice to desired thickness

Ceci Ripeni (Dessert)

Filling

- 4 cans of chick peas (aka—Garbonzo Beans)
- 1 lb of roasted and ground walnuts
- 2 grated orange skins
- 2 grated lemon skins
- 1/3 box of cocoa
- 1 Tbsp. of cinnamon
- 30 oz. of honey

- Boil, drain and mash chick peas
- Mix all other ingredients with chick peas

Dough

- 8 cups of flour
- 16 oz. of red wine
- 10 oz. of vegetable oil
- 4 Tbsp. of sugar

- Mix and make dough
- Cut dough to large ravioli size and fill with mixture like a very large ravioli
- Deep fry with Crisco (solid)

ABOUT THE AUTHOR

Rock DiLisio is from Pittsburgh, Pennsylvania (USA) and a first-generation Italian. Both his father and mother (Angelo and Alba DiLisio), as well as both sets of grandparents (Rocco and Maria DiLisio and Cosimo and Lucia DiGenova) were born and lived in the City of Sulmona, province of L'Aquila (Abruzzo) and a number of family members continue to reside in the city and Abruzzo region. His father once operated a travel agency in suburban Pittsburgh, near the Pittsburgh International Airport.

Rock's international travels have taken him through the Abruzzo towns and cities of Pescara, Scanno, Raiano, Pacentro and Sulmona, as well as cities and locations throughout Italy, such as Rome, Venice, Florence, Naples, Capri, Pompei, Sorrento, Ischia, Padua, Venafro, Caserta, as well as San Marino and Vatican City. He has also traveled around the world to destination cities such as Paris, France, London, England, Melbourne—and various parts of Victoria, Australia, as well as locations in Mexico and Canada. Rock has also traveled to many destinations throughout the United States.

Other books from Rock DiLisio include the French and Indian War based, *American Advance* and the World War II Chronicle, *Firings From the Fox Hole*. He is also the author of *Sherlock Holmes: Mysteries of the Victorian Era*, and the fictional archaeological-action/adventures series—*Three Kings of Casablanca* and *Stone of the Sahara*—with more in the series to come. His work has also appeared in various magazines, newspapers and periodicals.

Printed in the United States
by Baker & Taylor Publisher Services